The Breath of Life

A Simple Way to Pray

by Ron DelBene
with Herb Montgomery

WINSTON PRESS

Cover photo: Cyril A. Reilly

Cover design: Maria Mazzara

Library of Congress Catalog Card Number: 80-53555

ISBN: 0-86683-639-X (previously ISBN: 0-03-059059-0)

Printed in the United States of America

5 4 3

Winston Press, Inc., 430 Oak Grove, Minneapolis, MN 55403

To all those
who have shared their lives with me
in prayer

Contents

INTRODUCTION

My friendship with Ron DelBene has established itself through the years. When I first met him, Ron had a recently acquired master's degree in theology and the shiny look of inexperience. Like so many of his contemporaries who were coming of age in turbulent times, Ron had a lot to learn. But learn he did.

As early as 1960 Ron was seriously studying and practicing meditation. In the years that followed, he participated in Cursillos and the Renewal Movement and went on to give retreats for adults and young adults. Like a river, Ron was always moving on, developing a dynamic force and identity of his own. At each fork along the way he accepted what the Lord offered and continued his journey: teaching, researching, counseling, being part of a family with his wife Eleanor and their two children.

Although I encouraged him to write, Ron always had some reason not to. For a very long time he was more at home behind the speaker's podium than he was behind a typewriter. Eventually I realized that the give-and-take of many conferences and seminars in which Ron took part all across the U.S. was like climbing the steps on a ladder: He was gaining a broader view. I watched him blend experience with his formal education and thus add another dimension to his person—a dimension of understanding.

I've seen Ron's first gray hairs appear and listened to his dreams, and in this book I've had the privilege to call forth his understanding of a simple kind of prayer.

There are many people who hunger for prayer but do not know how to begin praying. They feel a bit embarrassed and aren't likely to join a prayer group or take a class. Others experience a nagging sense of unease because they know that their prayer life is not all it could be. This book will be of special help to these people as well as to all others who seek a form of prayer that is natural and simple. There is nothing forbiddingly formal or complicated about the breath prayer described in this book. It is a form of prayer that is growing ever more popular.

The genesis of the book goes back to the winter of 1979 when I visited the South for reasons I could not explain at the time. I'd had many opportunities to go before but had never taken them. So a question kept whirling in my mind—*why now?*

Often as a Christian writer I *know* that the time is right to begin a particular project. But for weeks I had been unable to connect various events that I felt should have some bigger meaning for me. Why had my mother recently revealed to me a long-kept secret about her prayer life? Why did so many of my conversations with strangers in restaurants and on the beaches lead to their sharing private spiritual experiences with me? Was there a common thread I did not recognize?

By the time I reached the DelBenes' home I felt uneasy and impatient. It was not a fearful uneasiness such as one might feel while waiting for a medical diagnosis. Rather, it was a sense that something important was about to happen, something that could easily be ignored or overlooked.

At the DelBenes', Ron was busy preparing for ordination to the Episcopal priesthood and Eleanor was anticipating the completion of her doctorate. In comparison, my trip seemed trivial. For a week, or longer, I would be staying in their "Hermitage." As a spiritual director, Ron works with people who come to the Hermitage. It was unusual that there just happened to be a vacancy when I made the trip on such short notice.

Although it is always good to renew a friendship, after a few days I began to feel that friendship might be the only reason I was so far from home and my own work. Perhaps the Lord had sent me away simply to be renewed and I was reading too much into recent happenings.

One evening, after the children had gone to bed, Ron, Eleanor, and I sat talking. Not recognizing anything in our conversation that would suggest a deeper purpose for my being there, I became restless as the hour grew late. Unwilling to call it a night, I pushed the conversation on. Ron yawned. Eleanor stole a glance at her watch. Morning would come all too soon for them and their children.

"Well," Ron said softly, "I could tell you something about the breath prayer—"

"That's it!" I broke in, recognizing the idea as clearly as a single dandelion on a spring-green lawn.

We talked only a little longer, but everything else said was anticlimactic. An idea had been born, and now everyone deserved rest.

Later, in the quiet of my room, I stared into the night where a sculpted figure of Francis of Assisi stood watch over the garden. I had the comfortable feeling that I, too, was being watched over. "Thank you, Lord," I whispered, "for the ideas that always come through." Then I fell asleep, knowing there was a lot of hard work ahead.

Now the work is completed, and the book is in your hands. I hope you enjoy what Ron DelBene has to say about prayer as much as I've enjoyed helping him say it. May the book add a new dimension to your spiritual life!

Herb Montgomery

1. WHERE DO WE BEGIN?

There are moments in life when we have the gift of knowing that God's time and our time intersect. These experiences are not so rare as some people would have us think. What is rare is having someone with whom to share the experience; someone with whom to reflect on the wondrousness of our God.

In beginning to look at our experience, it is important that we be honest with ourselves. Often things happen to us that have meaning which we cannot understand completely at the time. Yet *we know* that an event of unusual importance has occurred. We may be walking with a friend, or reading alone, or listening to nature when something alerts us. Like Moses at the burning bush, we proceed carefully, knowing that we are on holy ground. God's time and our time intersect, and we have the gift to know it.

My own life has included a number of such moments. As I share them with you, you may feel that some or all of them are quite ordinary experiences. Indeed, they may be, but while each of them was occurring I was aware of myself and my God in a mysterious and beautiful way.

I remember a Sunday evening one October when I realized that I had come to a point of unusual change in my life. God and I were especially close. *And I knew it.* I had a similar experience on another occasion as I prayed the words *Our Father* and began to weep.

I was an adult before I could share with anyone my experience as a young boy kneeling in a candlelit mission church in a small Ohio city. That child knew he had seen into heaven but dared not say so to anyone. God's time and his time had intersected, and the boy had the gift to know it.

Another experience occurred when I was older and saw a young woman standing at a distance in an archway. The overwhelming presence of beauty that I sensed has remained. That woman is now my wife Eleanor.

There is a common thread running through all my experiences where I have felt God's time and mine intersecting. In each of them my heart was touched, opened, and examined. At those times I "knew" what the Psalmist meant by the words "Yahweh, you examine me and know me" (Psalm 139:1). *I realized that both my mind and my heart had turned toward* God. That is prayer.

I ask you to look at your own life. What experiences have you carried secretly? Think carefully of those moments. Were you in some way on holy ground? Were you so touched by the event that you tucked it away in the privacy of your heart and dared not share it? It may be that such an experience is still something for which you hope.

This is where we begin. With our experiences—yours and mine. If religion is new to you, or prayer is new to you, or for any other reason you feel that your time and God's time have not intersected, be patient. The path described in this book is not the only path, but it is one that I and others have found helpful. We are pilgrims together on this path. On our journey to discover and practice a simple form of prayer—the breath prayer—we will quiet our minds and open our hearts to share reflections. And we will meet the Master.

Thoughts continue to jostle in your head like mosquitoes. To stop this jostling, you must bind the mind with one thought, or the thought of One only. An aid to this is a short prayer, which helps the mind to become simple and united . . . . Together with the short prayer, you must keep your thought and attention turned towards God. But if you limit your prayer to words only, you are as "sounding brass."

*—Theophane the Recluse, 19th-century monk, bishop, and spiritual director.**

* *The Art of Prayer: An Orthodox Anthology*, compiled by Igumen Chariton of Valamo, translated by E. Kadloubovsky and E.M. Palmer, edited with an introduction by Timothy Ware (London: Faber & Faber, 1966), p. 97. Reprinted with permission.

2. CALLED TO BE PRAYERFUL

A prayerful person is filled constantly with an attitude of turning towards God—in mind and heart and soul, and with the whole body (Deuteronomy 6:4-9). And at times when we are aware of this wholeness within ourselves we hear: "Be still, then, and know that I am God" (Psalm 46:11—*Book of Common Prayer*).

How am I to get myself together? How can I find the time to be still and know God? Certainly it is difficult in our busy society.

When people come to the Hermitage to enter into silence and prayer under my guidance, they often ask: "If I am to be silent, what will I *do*?" We have mistakenly equated silence with doing nothing. Or when someone is silent we often think something is wrong. Our heritage of prayer has perhaps given us this outlook.

Most of us who come from a Christian background have learned to say prayers, read prayers, listen to prayers, memorize prayers. We speak of mental prayer, of meditating, of thinking or studying prayer. But how often are we challenged to *become* prayer? How often are we challenged to believe that the very person we are can be a prayer to God and a prayer for others?

Do you know anyone about whom you can say: "He or she *is* a prayer"? If so, you know someone whose life speaks God. It is no longer the person but the living Christ we see (Galatians 2:20).

At this point, you may feel that to reach such a peak is impossible for those of us who don't feel that we see a saint when we glance in the mirror. It is not just others who are called to become prayer. No, the call is not just to a chosen few or a select group. You and I are called to be prayerful. Once we realize that, we look not to the peak which seems so distant, but to the present—the place where we live and love and interact with others in everyday life.

This prayerful person that we are called to be is one for whom Scripture is not merely something that tells stories of people and events long ago. Scripture is the living word that provides signposts for us. It is our guide along the path we follow.

Around us are many people who appear to have no sense of what they are doing in this life or where they are going. "Oh," they complain, "if only I could get myself together!" God wants us to get ourselves together. Our Creator calls us to be whole people, to be fully integrated people. Whole or integrated is what the word *perfect* means when used in Scripture: "You must therefore be perfect just as your heavenly father is perfect" (Matthew 5:48). God's call is not for halfhearted measures or wishes or dreams. The call for us is to be dynamic seekers. In seeking we find there is much more to us than we may have realized.

Prayer involves us in seeking, growing, loving. There is a danger, however, that in seeking we might become like the hunting dog that trees an animal and then stands at the foot of the tree yelping, jumping, and wearing himself out. We may believe that we have "treed" God. Then in our great excitement we wear ourselves out with a multitude of prayers that can easily become routine or even meaningless. If our prayers come from the mind only and do not reflect the integration of those prayers into our heart and whole being, we then mistakenly think that the mental action and vocal excitement give meaning.

Instead, perhaps we can be like the hunting dog that, after locating its quarry, stands still—pointing to the find. Although still, and "doing nothing," the pointer is alert and attentive. Through our attentive stillness, we can avoid what we might refer to as the "noise" of prayer and concentrate instead on the find which for Christians is the treasure, the pearl of great price, the Kingdom (Matthew 13:44-47). This is the ultimate will of God for us.

Unfortunately, many people view the will of God as rather like a ten-ton elephant hanging overhead, ready to fall on them if they don't make the right decision! Actually, the word which we translate into English as *will* comes from both a Hebrew and a Greek word which mean “yearning.” It is that yearning which lovers have for one another. Not a yearning of the mind alone or of the heart alone but of the *whole being*. A yearning which we feel is only a glimmering of the depth of the yearning of God for us.

With the breath prayer we will come to understand a little more fully how God’s love for us is a very clear invitation. An invitation to become prayer and one day be aware that we have joined God in the Kingdom. Everyone is invited.

Thus ceaseless prayer keeps our mental air free from the dark clouds and winds of the spirits of evil. And when the air of the heart is pure, there is nothing to prevent the Divine light of Jesus shining in it . . . .

—*Hesychius, an early 5th-century preacher and teacher of the church in Palestine, known for his knowledge of Scripture. From his writings to his friend Theodulus.**

* *Writings from the Philokalia on Prayer of the Heart*, translated by E. Kadloubovsky and G.E.H. Palmer (London: Faber & Faber, 1975), p. 315. Reprinted with permission.

God, you are my God, I am seeking you,
my soul is thirsting for you,
my flesh is longing for you,
a land parched, weary and waterless;
I long to gaze on you in the Sanctuary,
and to see your power and glory.

Your love is better than life itself,
my lips will recite your praise;
all my life I will bless you,
in your name lift up my hands . . . .

—Psalm 63:1-4

3. THE SCRIPTURAL BASE FOR UNCEASING PRAYER

In the Old Testament, Moses told the people of Israel never to forget the deeds of Yahweh, their deliverer.

> "Listen, Israel: Yahweh our God is the one Yahweh. You shall love Yahweh your God with all your heart, with all your soul, with all your strength. Let these words I urge on you today be written on your heart. You shall repeat them to your children and say them over to them whether at rest in your house or walking abroad, at your lying down or at your rising; you shall fasten them on your hand as a sign and on your forehead as a circlet; you shall write them on the doorposts of your house and on your gates." (Deuteronomy 6:4-9)

Today in our busy world we also need not to forget how God has saved us and made us whole. To have this remembrance always in our heart requires that we consciously seek to remember God's action in our lives. Moses was so concerned with this point that in the passage quoted he gave specific examples of ways people might post remembrances to help them recall God to their consciousness.

The letters of the New Testament speak about praying unceasingly and remaining in praise for the deeds God does in our lives. In Hebrews 13:15 we read: "Let us offer God an unending sacrifice of praise, a verbal sacrifice that is offered every time we acknowledge his name." In 1 Thessalonians 5:17-18, Paul the Apostle makes it clear that we should "pray constantly, and for all things give thanks to God." Colossians 4:2 reminds us to be diligent and "persevering in [our] prayers and be thankful as [we] stay awake to pray."

In peaceful as well as in troubled times we are called to respond to God's action in our lives—we are called to pray. In Romans 12:12 we are told: "Do not give up if trials come; and keep on praying." And in Ephesians 6:18 we find a similar directive: "Pray all the time, asking for what you need, praying in the Spirit on every possible occasion."

To pray without ceasing, on every possible occasion, means that *we are to be in a state of remembrance of what God has done and is doing for us*. We are to ask for what we need and to praise. In short, our prayer is to be one of praise and petition.

More than this, we are told to pray in the spirit, which can be more fully understood when we examine the Hebrew word *ruach* and its three translations: "wind," "breath," and "spirit." Time and again throughout Scripture we see God breathing life (Ezekiel 37:9-10 and John 20:22 are examples); we hear about God's wind blowing (Genesis 1:1 and John 3:8); and we learn of God's spirit entering into his people (Ezekiel 36:27 and Galatians 4:6).

Like the people of Israel, we need a way to remind ourselves to pray unceasingly. *Ruach*, the three-in-one word, gives us an insight to guide us closer to such prayer. And with the breath prayer itself we will see how praying "in the spirit given to us" and "in the breath given to us" can be made practical.

St. John of the Ladder advises: "Let the memory of Jesus combine with your breath—then will you know the profit of silence." Another teaches: "A monk should have memory of God in place of breath" or, as another says: "One's love of God should run before breathing."

—*Attributed to Gregory of Sinai, a leader in the spiritual-growth movement in the 14th century, a monk of Mount Athos.**

* *Writings from the Philokalia on Prayer of the Heart*, translated by E. Kadloubovsky and G.E.H. Palmer (London: Faber & Faber, 1975), p. 85. Reprinted with permission.

4. WHAT IS THE BREATH PRAYER?

The breath prayer is a short prayer of praise and petition. It is an ancient and natural form of prayer which is meant to help us become aware of the presence of God.

As we breathe unceasingly, that breathing supports life and renews our corporeal system. As we develop our ability to pray unceasingly with the breath prayer, God's love and life will support and renew us.

Remembering that *ruach* means wind, breath, and spirit, it is important to understand that while the breath prayer is a prayer of the breath it is also a prayer of the spirit. Of course in one very real sense we are always praying within to the Father; we know from Romans 8:26 that the Spirit is praying for us.

Just as breathing goes on naturally within our body without our consciously thinking about it, so prayer can go on naturally within our being. Thus the name "breath prayer."

Historically, the breath prayer rose out of

the Psalms. Repeated phrases are actually short prayers which remind us of the whole psalm.

In some religious traditions, forms of a breath prayer have been called "aspiratory" or "ejaculatory" prayers. The term *aspiratory* comes from the Latin word meaning "to breathe." The term *ejaculatory* comes from the idea of throwing a javelin. Such prayers have traditionally been short and have risen from individual need.

We most often use such short prayers in times of stress, need, or joy. We may pray: "Jesus, help me"; "O God, hear my prayer"; or "Praise be to Thee, O Lord!" Usually these prayers seem to rise spontaneously from within us, flowing out before we are aware of them. This is a natural experience.

As we look more closely at the breath prayer, we will see that it is a way to have on our lips what is always in our heart. It is such a simple way of prayer that many people have overlooked it. In our society, we tend to feel that if something is to be good, it must be complex. That is just not so.

It is said that Ignatius of Antioch, who was killed in the year 115 because of his faith in Jesus, used a short prayer over and over while in prison. When questioned by his jailers, who thought the words to be some kind of incantation, Ignatius explained that his teacher—who was John the Apostle—had taught him to have on his lips what was always in his heart.

Within the Christian tradition of the East there is a breath prayer called the Jesus Prayer which goes: "Lord Jesus Christ, Son of God, have mercy on me, a sinner."

In the sixth century there was a great need to create a disciplined form of prayer for the thousands of monks and other people who were seeking a deeper relationship with God. The Jesus Prayer was intended to be a kind of touchstone of the briefest form. It would compile and compress all the doctrine one needed to believe in order to be saved.

The Jesus Prayer was put together in the sixth century and was renewed throughout the Christian church in the East in the fourteenth and nineteenth centuries, most notably in Greece and Russia. *The Way of a Pilgrim*, a well-known book about and by an anonymous nineteenth-century peasant, contains a classic description of the use and beauty of this particular breath prayer.

Much has been written about the Jesus Prayer in recent years. Many people are adapting the practice of using either the traditional form, "Lord Jesus Christ, Son of God, have mercy on me, a sinner" or a shorter form such as "Lord Jesus Christ, have mercy" or even the extremely brief "Jesus, mercy."

Although the Jesus Prayer is a breath prayer, I prefer the individually discovered breath prayer for two reasons. First, it is the more ancient approach; more important, I believe that *a personalized prayer which arises from individual need clarifies who I am and thus helps me understand my relationship with God.*

There is an intimacy to the personal breath prayer that seems most suitable, since God calls each of us individually and invites us to grow into deeper union with him. Because each of us is unique, it seems appropriate that each of us also have our own special response to God. For me, the breath prayer is such a response.

So the breath prayer is a short, simple, ancient prayer of praise and petition. It is the truly personal response we make to God once we sense his loving invitation to draw nearer to him. Are you ready to accept his invitation?

When we come to any new form of prayer, it is helpful to learn from someone who has used the form for a long time. Even though we might not think we have a prayer within us, we do.

There is an often-repeated story about a gentle monk who was well known for his prayer life. Someone younger came to him and asked how he had reached the point where prayer was constant.

"Looking back," said the monk, "it seems that the prayer has always been deep in my heart. Once it was like an underground spring covered over with a stone. Then one day Jesus came along and removed the stone. The spring has been bubbling ever since."

5. HOW DO I DISCOVER MY BREATH PRAYER?

One of the beautiful things about the breath prayer is that it is yours, and now is the time to discover it.

One: Sit for a moment in silence and remember that God holds you in a loving presence. You may want to close your eyes and recall the words "Be still, then, and know that I am God" (Psalm 46:11—*Book of Common Prayer*) or ". . . when you pray, go to your private room and, when you have shut your door, pray to your Father who is in that secret place, and your Father who sees all that is done in secret will reward you" (Matthew 6:6).

Two: Listen as God calls you by name and asks: "______*(Your name)*______, what do you want?"

Three: Answer the Lord simply, directly.

Four: Write down your answer in the following space or on a separate piece of paper. You may write several responses if you have several answers.

In one group I was teaching, a woman blurted out after a moment of silence: "I just have to share what happened! I'm a secretary. When I closed my eyes, there I was sitting at my desk. Suddenly my typewriter went on and began typing my prayer on a piece of white paper, just as clear as anything." At that point, another person responded: "I didn't even hear a whisper!" So everyone is different and will have a different response.

The prayer usually rises out of our present concerns. One person may focus on physical health or healing, another on becoming still and peaceful within, another on learning to hear God's voice more clearly or to be released from guilt.

Now, you may be saying, "Why, I've been using a prayer like this, but I never thought of it as a breath prayer" or "I have this favorite line from Scripture [or a hymn] that has been with me." This is how natural the breath prayer is. Many have at some time used some phrase that has come back again and again. We have often sung it or let it roll through our mind. So we may not be talking about something new. The newness comes in doing this consciously and in working at seeing how we truly do want to respond to God.

What was your response to God's question?

Your answer may have been one word like *peace* or *love*. Or several words or phrases like *understand, feel, and know your love* may have come to you. Your answer, or answers, will become the foundation of your prayer.

Remember that the breath prayer is always a prayer of praise and petition. The praise comes from calling one of the divine names, such as Father, or Lord, or Jesus, or Master, or Christ, or God. This is then combined with a petition. We are never more childlike and humble than when we ask. Sometimes it is difficult to ask. We say we need nothing and only want to give thanks and praise to the Lord. Yet we recall Jesus' words "Ask and it will be given to you" (Matthew 7:7 and Luke 11:9) and "Whatever you ask for in my name I will do" (John 14:13).

Five: Select a name. What name do you usually call God? Father, Lord, Jesus, Master, God, Christ . . . ? Use the name of your choice, plus the word or words you wrote down, to make a short prayer of six to eight syllables. With *God* and *peace* you might pray, "Let me know your *peace*, O *God*." If your answer to God's question was that you want to be able to *understand* and *feel* and *know* God's love, then ask yourself which of these is most basic to you. If you believe that by understanding God's love you will then know and feel it, a good prayer could be: "Let me *understand* your love, Lord." If you believe that by feeling love you would then know and understand it, a good prayer could be: "Father, let me *feel* your love."

You may want to write two or three prayers as they come to you. Sometimes the first one written is clear and direct. At other times, we clarify our prayer by writing more than one.

People often ask, "If my breath prayer is so personal and rises out of my need, won't it change when my needs change?" The answer is yes. The prayer sometimes changes. It is important, however, when first discovering your personal breath prayer to have it be as basic as possible.

Look at your prayer. Does it reflect the very center of your need? Does it move you more deeply into the love of God? It should be personal and relate to your deepest need.

SAMPLE BREATH PRAYERS

Father, lead me into health.

Lord Jesus, let me be still.

Jesus, guide me in your will.

Let me know your presence, Lord.

Alleluia, have mercy, Jesus.

Let me come to you, Lord God.

Let me feel your spirit, Jesus.

Father, let me know your love.

Jesus, may your will be done.

Show me your way, O Lord.

Lead me in your light, O God.

Let your prayer be honest. One person wrote: "Jesus, Lord, come into my heart." We know from Scripture that Jesus has told us that he and his Father already dwell within those who love (John 14:23). What this person really meant by the prayer was that she wanted to *know* and *feel* Jesus in her heart. When the woman realized this, she changed her prayer to "Jesus, let me feel you in my heart." That was her personal need, her deepest desire, and an honest petition.

Let your prayer be rhythmic. A prayer of six to eight syllables will have a natural rhythm. Usually, anything longer or shorter does not flow as easily when said unceasingly. Changing words around may provide a natural rhythm. For one person, "Father, let me know your will" may have more rhythm than "Let me know your will, O Father."

Give your prayer a chance. As children of a society characterized by rapid change, we tend to be impatient and may want to change the prayer often. I suggest that you decide upon a prayer and then use it for a day or two, rearranging the words until they are personal and comfortable for you. But after this day or two, use the prayer unchanged for at least one month. This is another reason for making it as personal as possible at the beginning; a reason why we must listen to God calling our name and asking, "________ *(Name)* ________, what do you want?"

Recognize when it is time to change. You will know when it is time to change your prayer. People find themselves using a different prayer without even thinking. Often a change happens after a person has experienced a major insight or change in life situation. Birth, death, resolution of a problem, a new learning or discovery, a promotion—these are only some of the things that may shift the emphasis of your breath prayer. Callistus, a fourteenth-century spiritual teacher, says:

> . . . one should refrain from changing the words of the prayer too often lest this frequent chopping and changing [of attention from one thing to another] should accustom the mind not to concentrate on one thing but to deviate from it and so remain for ever not firmly planted in itself; and thus it will bear no fruit; like a tree which is many times transplanted from place to place.*

The next question comes quickly to mind. Now that you have a breath prayer, what do you do with it?

* *Writings from the Philokalia on Prayer of the Heart*, translated by E. Kadloubovsky and G.E.H. Palmer (London: Faber & Faber, 1975), p. 227. Reprinted with permission.

Let no one think, my fellow Christians, that only priests and monks need to pray without ceasing, and not laypeople. No, no: every Christian without exception ought to dwell always in prayer . . . . the Name of God must be remembered in prayer as often as one draws breath.

—*Attributed to Gregory Palamas, a 14th-century mystical writer on prayer.**

* *The Art of Prayer: An Orthodox Anthology*, compiled by Igumen Chariton of Valamo, translated by E. Kadloubovsky and E.M. Palmer, edited with an introduction by Timothy Ware (London: Faber & Faber, 1966), p. 87. Reprinted with permission.

6. LEARNING TO PRAY UNCEASINGLY

Learning to pray unceasingly is like learning any other good habit: It must be practiced. It takes discipline to continue practicing something until it becomes "second nature." When we first learn to knit, for example, every stitch is painstakingly done, and we check constantly to see if the stitch is right. But when we master the process, we can talk with others, watch TV and still go on knitting, seldom checking out or bringing into the forward part of our consciousness the fact that we are knitting.

Body work such as running or other exercise provides another example. When we first begin the discipline it is tedious. At times we wonder why we began. But there comes a point when we move beyond that constant attention and into a space of running or body movement where we flow with it. Our whole body moves with the rhythm. The inner person and the outer person are in harmony.

Begin to use your breath prayer, saying it as often as possible, in all places, under all circumstances. And remember to keep it at a slow pace. The purpose is to bring our exterior pace into harmony with our prayer, not to rush the prayer to match our exterior pace. Practice while walking—using half of your prayer on one step and the other half on the other step. Or walk slowly and say the whole prayer on each step. If you do some form of exercise or body movement, say the prayer in rhythm with your movement. Many people use a breath prayer while running, jogging, or swimming. Use it while washing dishes, making beds, getting dressed, going to sleep. Use it while driving, waiting in line, or when you find yourself impatient. There is no need to ever waste time again!

If you wish, say the prayer out loud when alone. Some people find themselves singing their prayer; others chant it aloud.

You may find it helpful in the beginning to change the emphasis on the words. This often provides striking insight into different aspects and nuances of the prayer. For example:

- *Father*, let me feel your love.
- Father, *let* me feel your love.
- Father, let *me* feel your love.
- Father, let me *feel* your love.

As you use the prayer more and more, it develops within you. *There is a process which begins with the oral stage.* You will sense the prayer being said and "residing," so to speak, in your mouth or throat. This is an essential part of the growth. Don't think it silly or vain repetition (Matthew 6:7). It is not. To call upon the name of the Lord and to ask as we have been commanded to do is not vain repetition but a constant response to God's great love for us.

Saying the prayer is important. Like any new habit, it demands that we remember to do it, and this is sometimes difficult. So it is helpful to set up a method to remind yourself to pray.

- A teacher prays every time a bell rings at school or the phone rings at home.
- A bank teller prays every time someone comes to his window.
- A woman whose favorite color is yellow prays whenever she sees something yellow.
- A doctor uses her prayer as she washes her hands before going on to her next patient and every time she enters a hospital room.
- Many people put pressure-sensitive labels or masking-tape reminders on the bathroom mirror, sink, refrigerator, phone, steering wheel, rear-view mirror.
- A lawyer put a sticker on his watch. Every glance at his watch reminds him to pray.

Whatever helps you establish the habit is worthwhile. The need for these reminders ceases when you enter more deeply into the disciplined life of prayer.

You will be reaching the second stage of the process when the prayer moves into the mind. One day you will find yourself saying the prayer and will realize that you were unaware of saying it. Or you will wake up in the morning and feel that you have been praying all night because the prayer is with you as you awaken. It is simply "there" and will move in and out of your consciousness. You will be walking and find yourself saying your breath prayer. You will be waiting in line or in traffic and find yourself saying the prayer. Then you know you are moving more and more into unceasing prayer.

The temptation at this stage is to sit back and enjoy the experience and think you have made it. But it is as important then as it was in the beginning to continue to pray consciously as often as possible. *The goal is to have interior thoughts and exterior actions become more and more integrated.*

It is at this stage that we ourselves—or the people around us—become aware of changes in our behavior. We no longer get so upset in traffic. We are more loving. We listen intently and have a more peaceful being. We feel that we are really growing in God. We enjoy silence more. We can be alone without fear. Difficult tasks seem to go more smoothly. We become aware that prayer is not just of the spirit and soul, but that it greatly influences our entire life.

During this time, if I were to ask where the prayer resides I would answer, "In my head." The prayer has moved into the mind and begun integrating all my thoughts. One young man said he found that a lot of the thoughts which had been troubling him were now gone because he had something else in his mind. God's work continues within us to transform us into his image and likeness.

The third stage of the process is when the prayer moves into the heart. This is a deeper integrating experience. As we pray with fervor and become more disciplined, the prayer moves from the mind into the heart. It is as if the mind itself has moved into the heart and there is now a union of the two. We think with love and make decisions based upon that love. This is definitely a time when our awareness of peace and love is increased. We find ourselves opening our hearts to others and becoming more conscious of praying for them as we recognize their suffering and joy.

In the last stage of the process, the prayer moves so totally into our lives that it moves into all members of the body. It is like our very blood or breath, moving from the lungs and the heart into all parts of our body and returning only to be pushed out again. The prayer has developed a rhythm so deep that it has become part of us. At this point, the prayer is united with our breath. It is truly part of our being.

Because we are all different, the time of each stage of the process will vary. These passages from stage to stage may take months and even years, so don't expect overnight success! There is, however, a secret to be discovered through praying unceasingly. The secret is that it doesn't matter where the prayer resides. Through the constant use of the breath prayer, change occurs. We become more attuned to God's new life and love and more aware that it is the Lord Jesus who lives in us and not we ourselves.

Friend, it is simple. Begin to pray your personal breath prayer. Repeat it at an even pace, over and over. There will be times when you feel that this is a silly or childish habit and that you cannot say the prayer another time. That is the time to say it twenty times more. Use your discipline to go on. It is worth it, for the time will come when you are praying unceasingly.

When the Spirit has come to reside in someone, that person cannot stop praying; for the Spirit prays without ceasing in him. No matter if he is asleep or awake, prayer is going on in his heart all the time. He may be eating or drinking, he may be resting or working—the incense of prayer will ascend spontaneously from his heart. . . . His thoughts will be prompted by God. The slightest stirring of his heart is like a voice which sings in silence and in secret to the Invisible.

*—Isaac the Syrian, 6th-century monk, bishop, and writer.**

* Reprinted with permission from *Teach Us to Pray* by Andre Louf, Franciscan Herald Press, Chicago, IL 60609.

7. MUST I GIVE UP OTHER FORMS OF PRAYER?

Remember that the Spirit has been praying within you all along. But now you have opened yourself in a new way and given words to what has been residing within. Being so conscious of the breath prayer and using it in a disciplined way makes it especially important for spiritual growth. But the breath prayer is not intended to take the place of the various forms of prayer you may already have been practicing.

I liken prayer life to a house that includes many parts, all of which require a foundation. Think of the place where you live. Each room serves a specific purpose in your life. While cooking in the kitchen, sleeping in the bedroom or gathering with friends in the living area, you give little thought to the supporting foundation. Unless, of course, it is faulty! Normally the foundation is there, doing the job for which it is intended. So it is with the breath prayer. It can serve as the foundation upon which a life of prayer is built.

Immediately after discovering your breath prayer, you will find it so new and exciting that it may be more like an addition to your home than a foundation. You will focus so much attention on the breath prayer that it may even seem to be a novelty. But as you become accustomed to your prayer, the newness disappears and its value as a foundation becomes apparent.

If the breath prayer is the beginning of a prayer life for you, it will form a foundation upon which you can build a house of prayer in the future.

It is essential that you continue in your own disciplined way to be a prayerful person. All forms of prayer bring us more and more into an awareness of living in the presence of God. Read Scripture, have time for intercessory prayers, do body movement, say your morning or evening prayers. But also practice getting the breath prayer into your daily routine so that you yourself discover its specialness.

There is a beginning and ending time for worship with friends and for participation in a prayer group and even for the personal readings on prayer which you may do. But the breath prayer is not limited to fixed times. It can be said anywhere and at all times, and it provides the link that holds together other activities which may be considered more formal prayer.

Many users of the breath prayer find it especially helpful in restoring or deepening calm so that they may give greater attention to other prayer forms. Two or three minutes of saying the breath prayer will usually provide this sense of peace. I urge you to try this for yourself, because, while it is a foundation, the breath prayer also helps to create a reservoir from which you can dip into the spring of living water. And there you will find serenity.

I have given up all my non-obligatory devotions and prayers and concentrate on being always in His holy presence; I keep myself in His presence by simple attentiveness and a loving gaze upon God which I can call the actual presence of God or to put it more clearly, an habitual, silent and secret conversation of the soul with God. . . . As for time formally set aside for prayer, it is only a continuation of this same exercise. Sometimes I think of myself as a block of stone before a sculptor, ready to be sculpted into a statue, presenting myself thus to God and I beg Him to form His perfect image in my soul and make me entirely like Himself.

—*From a letter of Brother Lawrence, a 17th-century lay Carmelite.**

* Excerpt (pp. 68, 70) from *The Practice of the Presence of God* by Brother Lawrence of the Resurrection, translated with an introduction by John J. Delaney, copyright © 1977 by John J. Delaney. Reprinted by permission of Doubleday & Company, Inc.

8. THE BREATH PRAYER BRINGS CHANGE

"Could it really be true that the Lord could hear me?" Steven wondered. "Could God ever hear my breath prayer, or is it just for me? Will I really, I mean *really*, know God? Maybe if I just say some magic words it will be true, but I can't remember any."

Steven had begun to use the breath prayer and was finding it difficult. This led him to a time of questioning everything. He did not yet understand that to wonder in the depth of ourselves is a beginning of a great journey. It is something we all move through.

At one time or another we, like Steven, may wish for the secret of the magic words to put us in union with God. There is nothing unusual about that, because we have become accustomed to living in an "instant" world. Although our perception might indicate that change occurs quickly, it seldom happens in a flash. Rather, the Lord prepares and gently tends us like a garden of rare plants. But we also have a part to play. We must be the gardener as well as the plant. We need to tend ourselves, and the breath prayer is the tool we use. Change and growth begin to happen, not by a flash of magic but through discipline and attentiveness to the presence of God in our lives. It does not happen in precise fashion on a particular day. Instead, there is a gradual move as we are led to be more perceptive of ourselves and of our relationship with God.

Perhaps the best way to describe the process of change that takes place within us as we enter into the discipline of using the breath prayer is that we begin to feel like a camel moving through the eye of a needle (Matthew 19:23-24). It is believed that Jesus, in comparing a rich man entering the kingdom to a camel going through the eye of a needle, was referring to one of the narrow gates of Jerusalem. Before a camel could go through the gate, the camel driver had to remove all that the camel carried. Unburdened, the animal could then pass through. The driver would then be busy for a time putting everything back on the camel.

We all carry around baggage that we feel we cannot do without. This baggage includes things, people, our past, our future. Some of these attachments are necessary and good. But the red flag should go up when we are *compulsively* attached to any of them. Compulsive attachments burden us and obscure life's importance. We read of extreme cases: one in which a person chose to be buried in a favorite car, another in which a son attacked his parents because of their smothering love. While these are extreme attachments, we all have lesser attachments and can benefit from changes that bring a greater balance to our lives. And unlike the camel, we have the option of staying unburdened.

In the following excerpt, we see how Robert's use of the breath prayer led him to an awareness of the need for unburdening in his life:

> I need to reorder some aspects of my life. I need to stop buying things and get out of debt. I need to start seeing Jesus in everyone. I need to care for my body and get going on some exercise. I need to bridle my anger. I'm becoming aware that it's like getting rid of a stubborn stain, and each time I wash it it gets lighter and lighter, but then I find another stain somewhere else.

Rose shared her reflections on life after settling into a regular use of her breath prayer:

> I was finding little things I *could* do without, and it made it so practical because they were things I'd been wanting to cut out for a long time, but the discipline of the breath prayer and my growing awareness of God's caring for me are making it easier.

We reluctantly begin to unpack our camel. And as we do, we discover that we do not even want to take all these things into the city of

Jerusalem with us. It is just like moving. The beginning stage of any move is to see what we can discard because we will not need it where we are going. That attitude underlies the entire change process. And the more we recognize our compulsive attachments, the more we can see ourselves as we really are. That is the second stage of the process—a growth in humility.

I believe humility is another word for honesty. Humility has sometimes been considered self-effacement and "putting oneself down," but it is not that at all. It is recognizing the truth about who we are before God and other people. Knowing who we are involves recognizing our fine points as well as our failures.

For a long period in my life, I was unable to accept a compliment. If someone said, "That's a beautiful shirt," I responded with some offhand comment about it being an old or cheap one. If someone told me my teaching was great, I laughed (a good defense, of course) and said, "Oh, I bet you always tell your teachers that." I was never able to humble myself to say a simple thank you and leave it at that.

I've never forgotten when I learned that lesson. It was in the fall of 1962 after a talk I had given in Cleveland, Ohio. It had been an exceptionally good presentation. A young girl named Mary came up to me. I remember what she wore, how she talked, where we stood. She said, "Ron, that was the most beautiful talk I ever heard. You moved something within me." I laughed self-consciously and said (and did really mean), "Oh, yes the Spirit of God does wonders." At that point Mary turned red and yelled at me, "That's the whole trouble with you Christians! Can't you take responsibility for anything? Can't you ever learn that we need to hear you say thank you! What makes you so special that you have to proclaim that the Spirit is with you? Are you afraid we won't see it?"

With the help of that girl's blunt words, I came to understand that I had been falsely making myself special by *not* accepting Mary's compliment. She needed me to say thank you to her, and that would have been my ministry to her. She needed me to recognize her as important, not immediately focus attention back on myself. I was good, and I needed to accept that fact. That experience helped me better understand that when we walk in the Spirit there is no need to proclaim it in loud words. Our being proclaims it.

Honesty also involves learning to say no when it is important to do so. I spent many years not saying no and then complaining about having to do what I had agreed to do. My work suffered, and I recognized that I was letting things control me rather than I controlling them. One reason I seldom said no was that I did not want to admit there were some things I did not do well or did not have the time to attend to. It was also a very subtle way to get people to pay attention to me and love me.

Most of the people with whom I share agree that coming to be able to say no is difficult. However, it is one of the essential things we must learn to do if we are to have time in our life to be replenished. Even Jesus said no to others in order to go away by himself.

After Tom began using the breath prayer and learned to say no to some activities in order to restructure his life, he described the change:

> Before, I was so busy doing all the good things that I had really forgotten to leave time to pray. I was using every second to plan my life and what I would do next. Now, using the breath prayer, I spend much more time being aware of living in God's presence, which I always was. I was just not as aware as I could be.

Perhaps the most difficult part of growing in prayer is understanding that where we are right now is where we are supposed to be. We can learn to live in the *now* of life rather than the tomorrows. After using the breath prayer for a number of years, Jane shared ideas that illustrate how one can grow to see the value of the here and now of life:

> My life relationships have become much smoother as a result of my efforts. I became more in tune with myself, my body, my work. I have become more loving and tolerant of people. I see them as having a beauty of their own. I live only periodically in that loved space, and have not given myself completely to God's love, but more and more each day I feel a letting go. I am between two worlds—desiring not to go back

> and yet unable to jump into the future. I am striving perhaps too hard for that total change, but I know that where I am now is where I am supposed to be. God loves me in the here and now. That is my place to love.

Continued use of the breath prayer over the years brings the awareness of a change in life-styles. There is no way we can remain the same when we move more and more into the presence of God. God's loving action transforms us. And of course the goal of all prayer is to make us more loving toward those with whom we live and work and play, for if we love them, then we are in fact loving God. This is the great insight we have from Paul the Apostle which formed the base of all his preaching and writing (Acts 9:1-6).

Change comes slowly; it sometimes appears not to be occurring at all. Be patient. You may be one of the many people who don't know where time goes and are often living such a rushed life that you feel the need to "catch your breath." This is not unusual. Because we live ahead of our breath so much, the use of the breath prayer at a slower pace begins to slow our external pace.

(By the way, this is also the reason why I neither emphasize nor even suggest trying to coordinate prayer with breath. Some people who live ahead of their breath hyperventilate—and get dizzy or light-headed—when they try to use the prayer in conjunction with their breathing. Do not try to match your prayer with your breath. Use your prayer slowly, almost gently, and after a time you will find that your own breath and the prayer have entered into a good pace together.)

Imagine a circle with its centre and radii or rays going out from this centre. The further these radii are from the centre the more widely are they dispersed and separated from one another; and conversely, the closer they come to the centre, the closer they are to one another. Suppose now that this circle is the world, the very centre of the circle, God, and the lines (radii) going from the centre to the circumference or from the circumference to the centre are the paths of men's lives. Then here we see the same. In so far as the saints move inwards within the circle toward its centre, wishing to come near to God, then, in the degree of their penetrations, they come closer both to God and to one another; morever, inasmuch as they come nearer to God, they come nearer to one another, and inasmuch as they come nearer to one another, they come nearer to God.

*—From a sermon delivered to his students by Abba Dorotheus, a spiritual director in the beginning of the 7th century.**

* *Early Fathers from the Philokalia,* translated by E. Kadloubovsky and G.E.H. Palmer (London: Faber & Faber, 1976), pp. 164-65. Reprinted with permission.

9. A TURNING POINT CALLED "THE GIFT OF TEARS"

Many people who use the breath prayer experience what is called "the gift of tears." It includes more than crying. The gift of tears is an experience of being overwhelmed by a sense of oneself in relationship to God. In this intimate and awesome state, we find ourselves crying, and it appears that there is no way to stop the flow. In this sense, there is a Mary of Magdala within each of us. We meet a Master who so evokes from us the total love we want to share that we lose control (Luke 7:36-38).

Like Peter, we are reminded of our unworthiness and our foolishness in turning away from and even denying the Lord, and we weep bitterly (Luke 22:60-62). Most of the time it is like a cloudburst; the floodgates open and we are deluged. This is how two of us describe the gift:

> When you suggested we pray together and said, "As our savior Christ has taught us we

are bold to say," I could feel a lump welling up in my throat and I didn't know whether or not I'd be able to pray. I blurted out, "Our Father" and then was overwhelmed with tears. (Ron)

I don't know what was happening, but I was just sitting in the car at the intersection waiting for the light to change and saying the prayer. All of a sudden I started to cry. I was so aware of how much God loved me. It only lasted a moment, but it seemed like I'd broken through into a new place to me. (Martha)

This gift of tears has been a turning point in people's lives not only in Scripture but through all the ages of Christianity. It is seen as an essential part of the growth process. Sometimes when we lose control and cry, we try to make light of it or dispel it. But there is no denying what has taken place. The following description of the gift of tears is an example of how an old self tried to fight off the new self (see Ephesians 4:22-24):

I then felt the beginning—the beginning of the new me, the beginning of the touch of the love of God. I felt appreciation, gratitude, and love. I then walked out into the rain, humble, and felt the rain and the cleansing comfort. There were small instances when my old Me came out and said, "This is foolish; this event is silly," but

> those feelings didn't stay very long because the old Me didn't have any lasting power. (James)

Through the gift of tears, the lasting power of living in the presence of God is turned into a sense of mission or ministry or caring for others. The person has a renewed interest in loving and a more intense desire for prayer. It is like a push through from one dimension to another where one senses a new light and a new way of living. It is a change in consciousness.

Often after such an experience the breath prayer changes. Edward had been using "Jesus, let me walk with you" as his breath prayer. One afternoon Edward asked to talk with me. We went for a walk around a nearby lake, and he began to unravel his concerns about anxieties and hostilities he felt toward some members of his family. As we were walking, Edward suddenly stopped. He seemed transformed as he looked at me and said, "You know, Jesus *is* walking with us, right now." I responded, "Yes, he is." The floodgates of Edward's eyes were opened then, and—as with Paul—scales of darkness, holding back insights into his life, fell away. The Spirit of truth was making Edward free. The pieces of his life and the mosaic of his relationship with God and his family came into place. We continued the walk in prayer as his tears flowed.

Later that evening, a worried Edward came to me. "I just can't seem to say my prayer any more," he said. "It doesn't seem to fit, for some reason." I asked him what prayer he had been saying. He responded, "Jesus, let me walk with you."

Even as Edward spoke, his eyes got larger and a knowing look came over his face. What awe there was in his voice as he said, "But I already have! When we walked around the lake, I experienced walking with him."

I suggested that the time had come to sit in silence for a bit and another prayer would be known to him because now he would have another answer to God's invitation: "Edward, what do you want?"

Edward's acceptance of the gift of tears moved him to serve others in greater love. The living presence of God became a more conscious part of his life.

It may be that you, too, will experience the gift of tears while using your breath prayer. If so, know that it is a sign of growth and development.

Then I am going to take you from among the nations and gather you together from all the foreign countries, and bring you home to your own land. I shall pour clean water over you and you will be cleansed; I shall cleanse you of all your defilement and all your idols. I shall give you a new heart, and put a new spirit in you; I shall remove the heart of stone from your bodies and give you a heart of flesh instead. I shall put my spirit in you, and make you keep my laws and sincerely respect my observances. You will live in the land which I gave your ancestors. You shall be my people and I will be your God.

—*Ezekiel* 36:24-28

10. THE BREATH PRAYER BECOMES PART OF LIFE

Some beautiful new houses were built at the end of our street, but as they sat there in the middle of their lots surrounded by dirt recently leveled and graded, there was something incomplete about them. The houses just did not fit the setting. In time, the grass grew and filled in the brown dirt with green, and some plants were placed near the foundations of the houses. Then one day I realized that now these beautiful houses fit in. They were no longer unattached. They had become joined to the surroundings and flowed into the landscape.

Because we pray only at certain times, our prayer can be like those houses: beautiful, but set apart from our living pattern. Then along comes breath prayer, like the grass and the plants. It joins not only all our other prayers but also the varied bits and pieces of life. We feel more whole, and we are.

As we practice praying unceasingly, the periods of time when we are not conscious of living in God's presence become fewer and fewer. We live more like his child, sharing in his glory (Romans 8:14-17). We walk more and more in the light and have less to fear because even in the dark we can see (John 1:4-9).

Making the breath prayer part of life requires discipline. Friends with whom I have shared in spiritual direction kid me about discipline because they have heard me say over and over, "Discipline is the key."

It is not hard to pray when we feel moved by the Spirit. It is not hard to pray when we are in a good mood or things are going well. It is not hard to pray with people who agree with us and pray as we do. It is not hard to pray at worship or when reading Scripture. But remember we are called to more than that; we are called to become prayerful people. To pray always in the Spirit, in the breath of God. And the more we become aware of our call, the more we become aware that our breath and the breath of God are becoming one.

To begin to consciously place ourselves in the presence of God is to begin to become a prayerful person. So when you feel an urge to say an unkind remark, say your breath prayer to yourself instead. When you feel a need to top someone's story, say the prayer. When you find yourself getting angry for whatever reason, say the prayer. Pray when waiting at the stoplight or for an appointment. Pray while hugging the children or teaching the class. Center on your breath prayer while you do the dishes or paint the house. Turn off the radio when you drive, and say your breath prayer instead. Abandon the TV after dinner. Go for a walk and pray.

Soon you will find yourself not only saying the prayer within yourself but also beginning to feel the overflow of love from your prayer going out to other persons. This can become a very deep form of intercessory prayer.

People who seriously use the breath prayer often find themselves more drawn to silence than before. Some even experience a need to withdraw from time to time to be alone. This is natural. It is a stage we move through; a stage when we integrate more and more into our life. Many of us spend most of our time with others. We are like a pendulum stuck to one side, out of balance. We need to be alone and in silence, and the breath prayer can become the balancing force. So don't be concerned if you find yourself wanting to spend more time alone or if you realize a need for a few minutes of silence each day. To rebalance your schedule, enter silence and pray. For some people this is an almost foreign experience; that is how accustomed we have become to the hubbub of activity.

As you use your prayer unceasingly, you will find the pace changing. Your external pace will begin to slow down and a greater integration or flow will take place. You will become more in tune with your body, your whole self, and your work. You will find yourself being freed from things and from people to whom you had compulsive attachments. You will become more honest about your abilities and your life. You will be more patient and may have your horizons widened or shifted.

Each of us has a horizon upon which we base many of our actions. It is the familiar base from which we operate. As long as that horizon or base is there—and we see it—, we can get our bearings to go about life. But when we lose that horizon, we are set off balance. We need to reestablish our horizon (after a death, a birth, the loss of a job, a dramatic discovery, learning or insight, a thirtieth or fortieth birthday, graduation), and usually the horizon is a new one.

Any good friend or teacher reassures us that the present horizon is what it should be for where we are right now, and at the same time that friend or teacher encourages us to move onward. The breath prayer really does widen or shift the old horizon for people who practice it. There is a whole new world of possibilities! That is why it is important to have someone with whom to share aspects of our spiritual growth. We grow not as individuals alone but as individuals within a community.

Although it may be difficult to find someone with whom to share the meaning of your breath prayer, look for such a person. Give a copy of this book to a close friend or to a person you would like to have as a friend. Look at teachers, counselors, ministers or leaders you know, and see if you are drawn to one of them. Perhaps you could join or form a group to study prayer. Seek to establish a relationship in which you can communicate your feelings about the spiritual direction you are taking.

The breath prayer provides a meeting ground for people. Though each person has his or her individual prayer, each knows that the other is praying unceasingly. When I go into a group and recognize someone there who I know uses a breath prayer, I sense a oneness that is a good and warming experience.

Near our home was a post office that was notorious for its long lines at the lunch hour. I may overuse the idea of praying while in line simply because of my numerous experiences of doing so at this post office! But let me share an example of "togetherness" that happens to people using their prayers. As I was in line one day, I glanced up and saw Barbara in the other line. She had attended one of my classes to learn about the breath prayer. Our eyes met and she smiled as she said, "I know what you're doing, and I bet you know what I'm doing." That was all that was said. We both laughed and continued waiting in silence, in prayer.

The breath prayer involves us in becoming prayerful persons in the ordinary stuff of life. Wherever we are, we are conscious of the presence of God in the midst of his people. Use your breath prayer at all times and in all places. Very soon you will realize that it has become a part of your life, an important part.

Unceasing prayer consists in an unceasing invocation of the name of God. Whether talking, sitting, walking, making something, eating or occupied in some other way, one should at all times and in every place call upon the name of God, according to the command of Scripture: Pray without ceasing. . . . (I Thessalonians 5:17)

We must pray with the heart; we must also pray with the mouth, when we are alone. But if we are in the market, or in the company of others, we should not pray with the lips, but only with the mind.

*—Kallistos, a Byzantine spiritual writer, 14th-15th century.**

* *On the Prayer of Jesus: From the Ascetic Essays of Bishop Ignatius Brianchaninov*, translated by Father Lazarus (London: John M. Watkins, 1965), pp. 60-61. Reprinted by permission of Watkins Publishing, Dulverton, England.

11. A SPECIAL PLACE AND TIME FOR PRAYER

In addition to praying always while doing whatever we are doing, there is also a need for a special place and time for prayer. *I want it to be clear that the length of time is not as important as the taking of that time.*

What we are going to do now is called "sitting prayer," because that is exactly what we do—sit and say the breath prayer, entering into a more intense time of being in the presence of God. This is a great discipline to develop.

Have you ever sat in silent prayer? If not, start with five minutes. Or if you are used to sitting in silence, begin with ten minutes. There is nothing fixed about these times, so feel free to do whatever is comfortable. Be aware, however, that it is important not to set a lengthy time for yourself simply because you are excited by the thought of beginning something new. It is better to do five minutes in a regular way than twenty minutes today and five tomorrow and then ten the next day. *More is not better.*

The key to success in sitting prayer is discipline. There will be days when you look forward to the sitting-prayer time, and there will be days when you wonder why you cannot sit still. In this sense, prayer becomes like training for the race that Paul speaks about (1 Corinthians 9:24-27). You cannot train one day, then be off awhile, train again, then neglect yourself and still expect to reach your goal. You need a schedule and the inner discipline to adhere to it. Here is where sharing with a friend or a group can be a great help and support.

The place where you do your sitting prayer is also important, so create one. Find a place where you can be "at home" in prayer. It is preferable to use a straight-back chair or to sit on the floor or on a cushion. The spot you select might be a corner of a room where you can have a picture or a Bible or a candle or something else that makes the place special to you. If you are fortunate and have an unused room, make that your special place. People can be creative in finding space. One woman cleaned out a closet and then put her Bible and a favorite picture on one of the shelves. When it is time for her sitting prayer, she opens the closet door, moves a chair in front of the closet, and has her special place.

A professional man does his sitting prayer when he arrives at his office. He merely opens his closet door and sits quietly in front of an icon he has hung on the door.

Many people create their special place at a dining-room table. Each time they sit down to pray, they open the Bible and light a candle.

Look around the room where you plan to do your sitting prayer. Create a special nook where you can go for your time in prayer.

Ritual is important, and I suggest having a plan to follow so that our time in prayer becomes a little more special. Usually when we get ready to do anything special we go through some ritual. We get dressed up to go out. We have birthday and anniversary rituals. We even make special preparations before sitting down to watch a long movie or ballgame on TV. The following ritual for the sitting prayer is to help us become more aware that this is a special time for us in God's presence.

One: Wash your hands. The hand-washing can be a reminder of a passage through water which, in Scripture, is seen as a transition into a new way of life or ministry to others (Exodus 14:15-31, Ezekiel 36:24-29, Matthew 3:16-17). It can also remind you of your own baptism. We come to prayer because we are called into the healing and living waters in the Spirit.

Two: Set a timer for the length of time you wish to sit in prayer. I suggest using a timer (on the stove, or any timer) so that it will be unnecessary to interrupt your prayer to look at a watch or clock. There will be days when the five minutes you sit will seem like one minute. There may also be times when you are certain you have prayed a half-hour but find you haven't! (By the way, if the sound of the timer seems loud, move it—or yourself—to another room.) It is important not to have to keep track of time. Let the timer do it, so you can be peaceful.

Three: Read a verse from Scripture. This is a reminder that we are fed through the constancy of God's Word. Read only a verse or line. I suggest the Psalms or John's Gospel because of the quickness with which we can find a meaningful line or verse there. The purpose is not to ponder the verse but to place ourselves more intently in the presence of God.

Four: Sit in prayer and slowly repeat your breath prayer in rhythmic fashion. Over and over and over. If you find yourself thinking about other things, know that you are normal. Don't worry about other thoughts. When you are aware of them, just come back calmly to the prayer. (We do begin to see how undisciplined we are, though, when we cannot even concentrate on one thing for a few minutes.)

Some people find it helpful to begin the sitting time by saying the breath prayer out loud a few times, saying it ever more softly until they become more and more silent within themselves. Again, remember that we can change the emphasis of the words in the prayer. This sometimes helps us remain attentive.

The sitting-prayer time is a time to become attentive to God, not passive. The writers of the early centuries talk about the prayer bringing calm attentiveness. Like the hunting dog mentioned earlier, be still but perfectly attentive.

Set a time that is good for you, and plan to sit daily. The morning is better for most people only because then the action is taken care of for the day and does not get pushed aside by other things.

So—find a time that is good for you, create a special place, and be a faithful person.

Father Chariton, a spiritual teacher early in this century, wrote something that I believe is helpful to read before each sitting time.

> You must never regard any spiritual work as firmly established, and this is especially true of prayer; but always pray as if beginning for the first time. When we do a thing for the first time, we come to it fresh and with a new-born enthusiasm. If, when starting to pray, you always approach it as though you had never yet prayed properly, and only now for the first time wished to do so, you will always pray with a fresh and lively zeal. And all will go well.*

* *The Art of Prayer: An Orthodox Anthology*, compiled by Igumen Chariton of Valamo, translated by E. Kadloubovsky and E.M. Palmer, edited with an introduction by Timothy Ware (London: Faber & Faber, 1966), p. 74. Reprinted with permission.

I urge you, then, pursue your course relentlessly. Attend to tomorrow and let yesterday be. Never mind what you have gained so far. Instead reach out to what lies ahead. If you do this you will remain in the truth. For now, if you wish to keep growing you must nourish in your heart the lively longing for God. Though this loving desire is certainly God's gift, it is up to you to nurture it. . . . Press on then. I want to see how you fare. Our Lord is always ready. He awaits only your co-operation.

*—From one of the letters of an unknown spiritual director of the 14th century.**

* *The Cloud of Unknowing*, edited by William Johnston (Garden City, New York: Doubleday Image Book, 1973), p. 47. Reprinted with permission of Doubleday & Company, Inc.

12. A JOURNAL FOR REFLECTION

One of the best ways to reflect upon our prayer is to keep a simple journal. After each sitting prayer, take three to five minutes to write in a notebook or diary what you have experienced. *This is not meant to be a tedious task!* Simply write the date, the time of day, and at least two sentences about what happened during your prayer. You might jot down the thoughts you had, experiences you recalled, emotions you felt, or physical reactions you had. Such journal-keeping is an easy way to remain faithful to growth and to a discipline. Journal entries also reveal changes much the way a family photo album does.

Friends have given me permission to share entries from their journals to show what kinds of things have been written. These are early entries made by people during their first weeks of using the breath prayer.

> This journal kept getting in my way. Will I remember what to write down? All the

outside sounds kept coming in—do the birds always chirp so loudly in the A.M.? Does the dog always breathe so heavily? A few really quiet seconds of a peaceful feeling. And wonder of wonders, was 10 minutes really so short! (Rebecca)

I am very quiet. Even to write seems an effort. I write slowly. Fifteen minutes seemed to have passed pleasantly and quickly. I was reluctant to stop. After perhaps five minutes I became very still, began to pray silently instead of out loud. My mind kept up an observing commentary, but the stillness surrounded all. The phone rang and I knew I would not rise from my prayer to answer it. (Mary Ellen)

Felt very calm and peaceful. Found that my mind was wandering or blank and so I went back to the prayer. Felt calmer and more relaxed. My mind did not seem to wander as much. (Peter)

I became aware as I sat in prayer that I've known for some time that the power moving me in the direction I have been going the past four or more years was more powerful than I am. The Spirit that is moving me will not let me stop. The pages will continue to be turned and the traveler will go on by whatever mode of transportation. (Jack)

Saying "Jesus, let me hear your voice." What am I asking? Am I ready to hear him? Ready

> to do whatever he asks of me? This is rather frightening. I know myself so well—will it be something I can't give up? I am weighing the question. (Stephanie)

Remember, keep your journal simple. Make journal-keeping part of the ritual of the sitting-prayer time, but limit writing time so you aren't overwhelmed by it. Usually three to five minutes is sufficient. Of course you may write in your journal longer or at other times if you wish, recording dreams or any experiences you want to include. The goal, however, is always to write after each sitting-prayer time.

Do you already keep a journal of some sort? Then incorporate your sitting-prayer reflections into that journal and key them in some way so they are easy to find at any time in the future.

The sitting-prayer ritual becomes a time for reflection about who we are in the presence of God.

RITUAL FOR SITTING PRAYER

One: Wash your hands to remind yourself of your passage into a new way of life or ministry.

Two: Set the timer for the period you will be sitting.

Three: Read a verse from Scripture, recalling again God's presence with you.

Four: Sit in prayer.

Five: Write in your journal when you have finished.

How dear to me is your dwelling, O Lord
of hosts!
My soul has a desire and longing for the
courts of the Lord;
my heart and my flesh rejoice in the
living God.

The sparrow has found her a house and the
swallow a nest where she may lay her young;
by the side of your altars, O Lord
of hosts,
my King and my God.

Happy are they who dwell in your house!
they will always be praising you.

Happy are the people whose strength is
in you!
whose hearts are set on the
pilgrims' way.

—Psalm 84:1-4
(Book of Common Prayer, 1979)

13. WHAT HAVE OTHERS EXPERIENCED?

I have asked people who have used the breath prayer for varying lengths of time to share what they have experienced. They responded by telling me that they would like you to know about these personal observations:

> I've been using the breath prayer for a little longer than a year now, and I think the most important thing I've come to see is how closely my body is connected to my prayer. When I first began to use the prayer, I was tense and full of aches and pains when I did the sitting. Just sitting still was hard for me. I was always running. But I am continuing to slow down, to feel better and to be more aware of how important it is for me to be aware that my body is a gift from God. (Mary)

> I am a counselor and after using the breath

prayer for over two years, I find that I am able to use it in my practice more and more. I look at my clients and pray for them. I find I am more insightful and rely more on the promptings within me in my work. I know I am more loving. (Steven)

I was forged in the fiery furnace, melted down in the flames of pain and lost in agony and fear and knowledge of my nothingness till all that was left was a spark, a tiny cinder. God breathed life on that spark till it became an eternal flame and I was born. (Marie)

One great truth that has overwhelmed me is that while we can approach God as a loving Father, he is still sovereign over all. It is with awe and trembling that we receive this privilege. It was not cheap grace but a profound awareness of a level of existence more profound and powerful and bold than one could in human thought imagine. (John)

Leading the congregation in worship has changed for me since I have been using the breath prayer. I find myself praying during the silent periods. I find that I am more centered and at peace when I celebrate the worship. (Richard)

It's been a long process, and I've wanted to quit many times. But there was something in me that just said, "Don't." So I didn't.

> There has been much pain in seeing myself as I really was, but there has also been much joy. I feel most that I wish I had more people to share this great joy with. (Theresa)

> My life with God has been transformed. Praying unceasingly has led me into a state I never thought possible. To be in the presence of God and to be aware of that is a great gift. Praise be to God! (Sam)

Although your experiences may not be the same as the experiences others have shared, the God who moves in and among us is the same. His action is seen differently through different eyes, but his action is the same. So it is that we are united in our common life in the Spirit and individually seek to grow more and more alive and conscious of the living presence of our God.

Each of us is called by name and asked: "What do you want?" And each of us answers in his or her own way. As God unceasingly invites us to enter into his yearning love, we have the opportunity to respond unceasingly.

We often feel unworthy, and in some sense we are. Who are you and who am I but little grains of sand upon the beach among so many? Yet we have been called, and that makes us special. We have been called where we are—weak, not yet perfect, sometimes seeing ourselves as unlovable. But that is the great mystery of God—that in his infinite humor he has chosen to love you and to love me.

I invite you to join the growing number of

people who are committed to unceasing prayer. Discover your breath prayer, practice it until it becomes a part of your everyday actions. Do so and you are sure to experience God's love in ways you never expected as you follow your own life path.

The principal thing is to stand with the mind in the heart before God, and to go on standing before Him unceasingly day and night, until the end of life.

—*Theophane the Recluse, 19th-century monk, bishop, and spiritual director.**

* *The Art of Prayer: An Orthodox Anthology*, compiled by Igumen Chariton of Valamo, translated by E. Kadloubovsky and E.M. Palmer, edited with an introduction by Timothy Ware (London: Faber & Faber, 1966), p. 63. Reprinted with permission.

RON DELBENE, an Episcopal priest, is rector of Holy Cross Church in Trussville, Alabama, and director of The Hermitage, a center for individually guided spiritual direction. DelBene also travels extensively, conducting conferences and retreats for training church leaders to teach the breath prayer in their parishes.

HERB MONTGOMERY, who resides in Minneapolis, Minnesota, is the author of numerous religious teaching aids, short stories, articles, and inspirational books.